THIRTEEN FOLKSONGS
PERCY GRAINGER
VOICE AND PIANO

Cover Photo: G. Schirmer, Inc.

ED-3744

G. SCHIRMER, Inc.

DISTRIBUTED BY

HAL•LEONARD®
CORPORATION
7777 W. BLUEMOUND RD. P.O. BOX 13819 MILWAUKEE, WI 53213

Contents

Pronunciation Guide

å = *a* in German hat

ä = *a* in father

ã, ãy = *a* in bare

â, o = *aw* in awe, *o* in for

ė = *er* in her
(but without the r sound)

ē = *ee* in green

ī = *i* in pine

ô = *o* in nor

ö = *o* in food

ǫ = *o* in cod

õ = *o* in note

ó, ů, ȯ̇ = *u* in put

ṙ = so-called "blurred r," that is, the *r* is mute and the tip of the tongue "inverted" (curled up and back) pronouncing the foregoing vowel.

"WILLOW WILLOW."

for Roger Quilter.
Mo te hoa takatapui.

Voice and Piano version.

Impulsively and very feelingly

3. Take this for my fare - well and lat - est a - dieu, Sing

wil - low wil - low wil - low, write this on my tomb,____ that in

love____ I was true. O wil - low wil - low wil - low wil - low, O

wil - low wil - low wil - low wil - low shall be my gar -

THE TWA CORBIES

Scotch folk-poem from Sir Walter Scott's "The Minstrelsy of the Scottish Border"

set for

a man's voice (high middle) and 7 strings (2 violins, 2 violas, 2 'cellos, 1 double-bass)

by

PERCY ALDRIDGE GRAINGER

Composed Feb. 25 — 28, 1903, London
Scored Nov. 24, 1909, London

No musical material of a traditional origin is used in this composition

Version for voice and piano

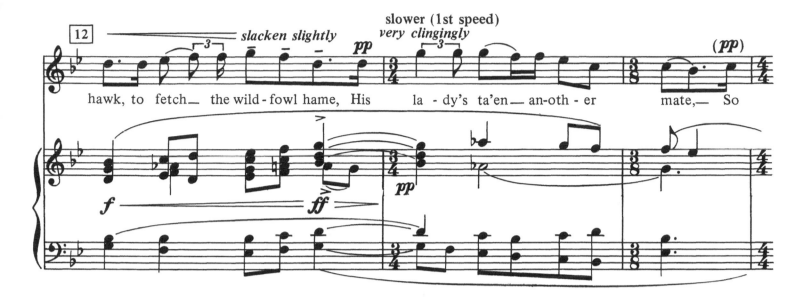

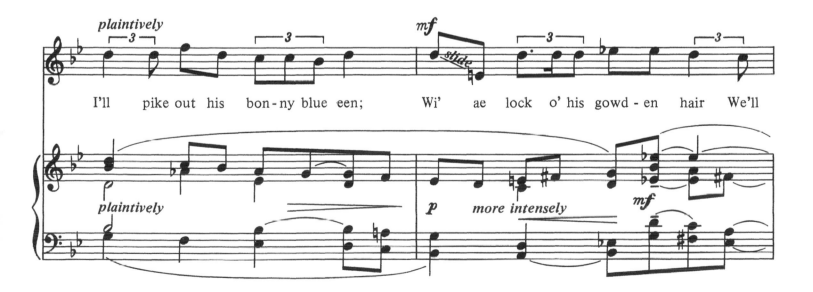

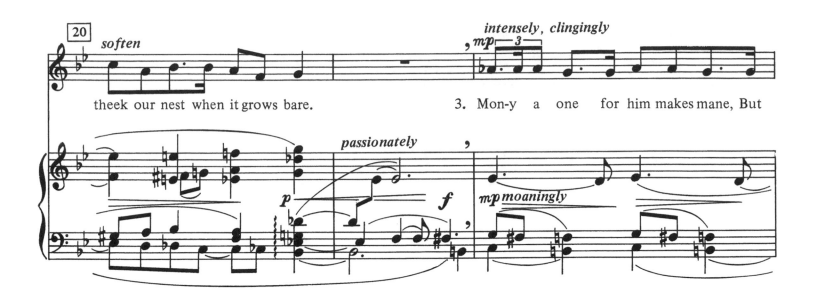

theek our nest when it grows bare.   3. Mon-y a one for him makes mane, But

nane sall ken whare he is gane: O'er his white banes, when they are bare, The wind sall blaw for ev - er-mair."

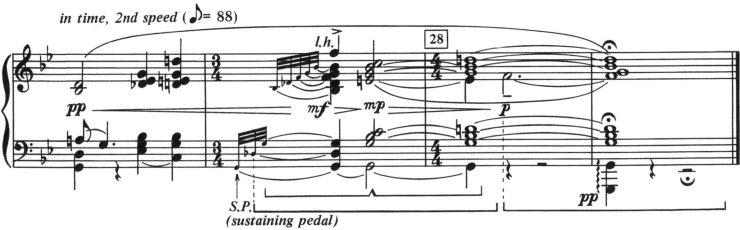

PERCY ALDRIDGE GRAINGER.
BRITISH FOLK-MUSIC SETTINGS.

(Lovingly and reverently dedicated to the memory of Edvard Grieg.)

Nr. 10. "DIED FOR LOVE."

May be key-shifted (transposed).

Score, or voice and piano version.

Tellingly, and with rhythmic stress, athough not loudly.
Quite simply, and with tender gaiety.
Not dragged, and strictly in time throughout.

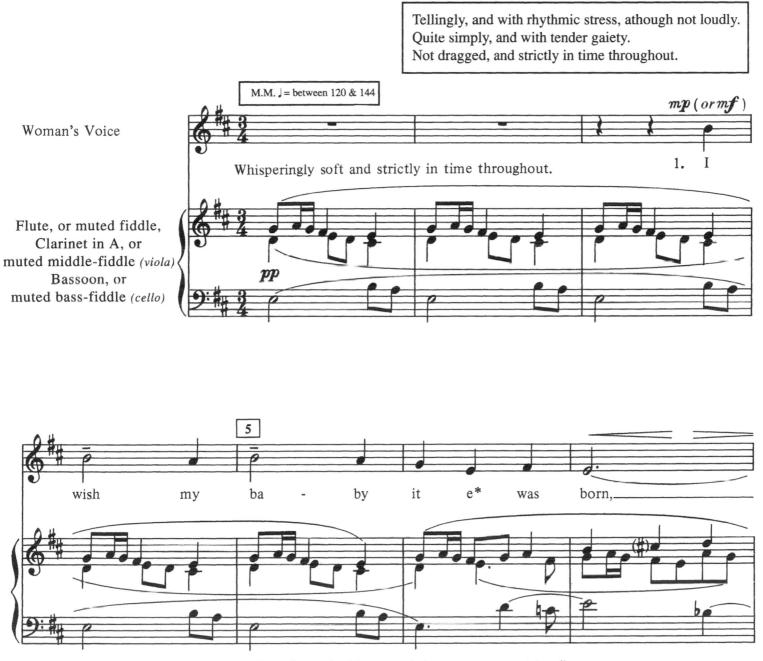

*"e" is a folksinger's added "nonsense syllable," and should be sounded just like the word "err."

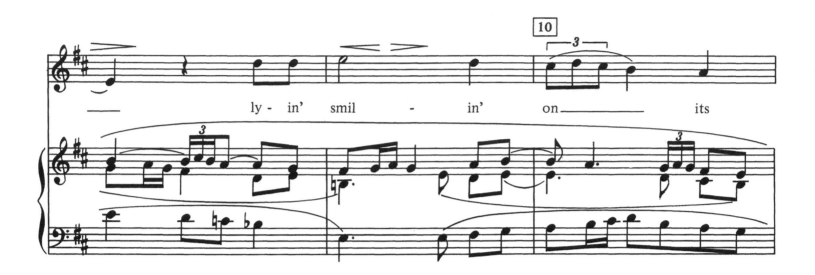

ly - in' smil - in' on_____ its

fa - ther's knee,_____ *add - nd(and)

I was dead_____ and in my

*"add-nd" should rhyme with "maddened."

grave, _____ and green _____ gress (grass) grow - in' all

o - ver me. _____

2. Dig me my grave long,

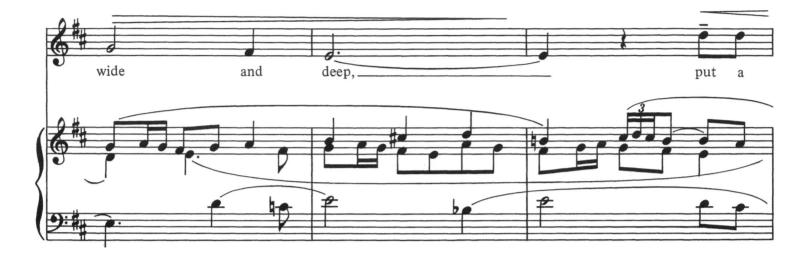

wide and deep, _____ put a

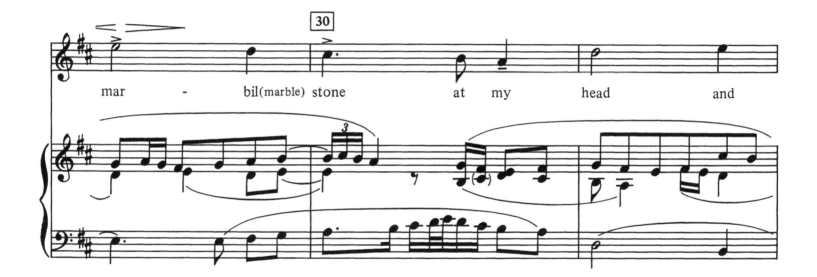

30

mar - bil(marble) stone at my head and

slight (poco)

feet; _____ *1 but a *2 tur - tle white

*1-4 sound the "u" in "but" and "turtle" and the "o" in "above" and "love" like the "u" in "put", "butcher."

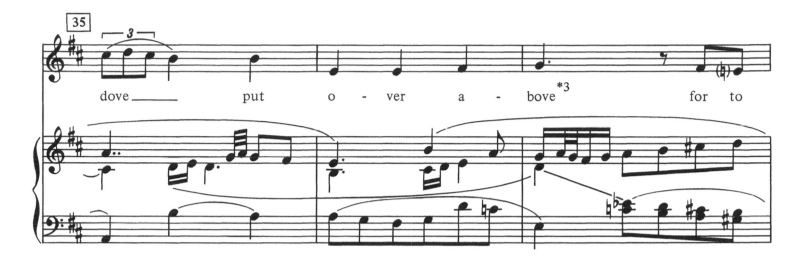

dove _____ put o - ver a - bove *3 for to

let the world know that I died _____ for

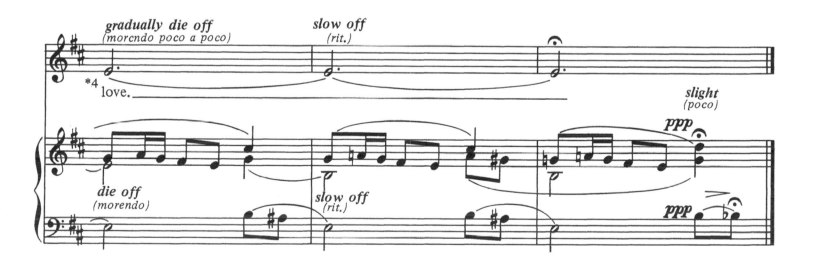

*4 love. _____

PERCY ALDRIDGE GRAINGER.
BRITISH FOLK-MUSIC SETTINGS.

(Lovingly and reverently dedicated to the memory of Edvard Grieg.)

Nr. 11. "SIX DUKES WENT AFISHIN'."

set for voice (woman's or man's) and piano.

For my friend Gervase Elwes.

Version for high voice.
May be key-shifted (transposed.)

VERY SIMPLY AND WITH A CHILDLIKE PATHOS.
Not too slowly. M.M. ♩ = about 76.

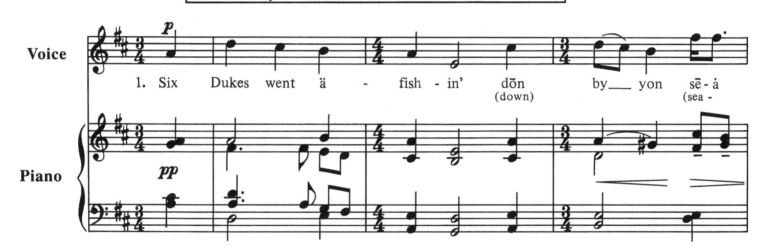

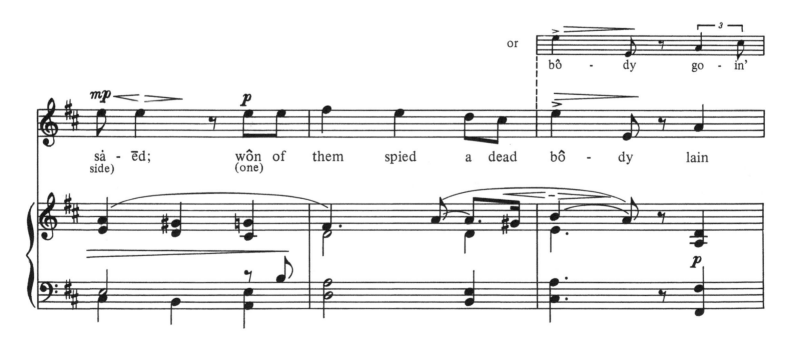

or

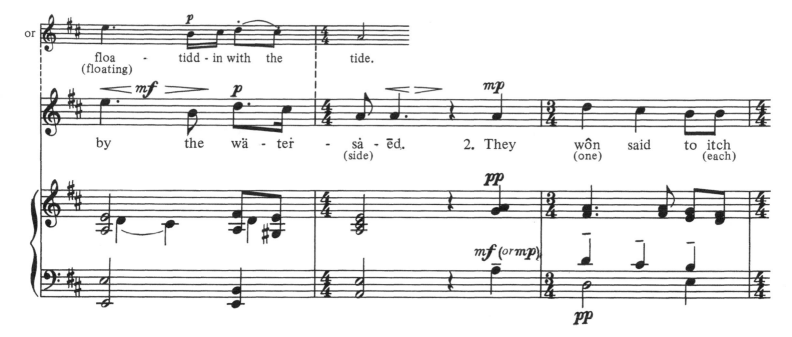

floa - tidd - in with the tide.
(floating)

by the wä - teṙ - sȧ - ēd. 2. They wôn said to itch
(side) (one) (each)

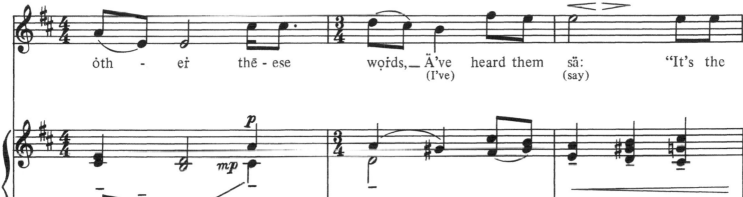

òth - eṙ thē - ese woṙds,— Ä've heard them sä: "It's the
(I've) (say)

Rô - ē - yull Duke of Grant - 'am what the tide 'às ė weshed a -
(Royal) (Grantham) (has washed)

warmly
(sonore)

keep it delicate
(sempre delicato)   *slight (poco)*

nō̄_____ lies   in   cold   clä,_____   when the
(now)   (clay)

richer
(più sonore)

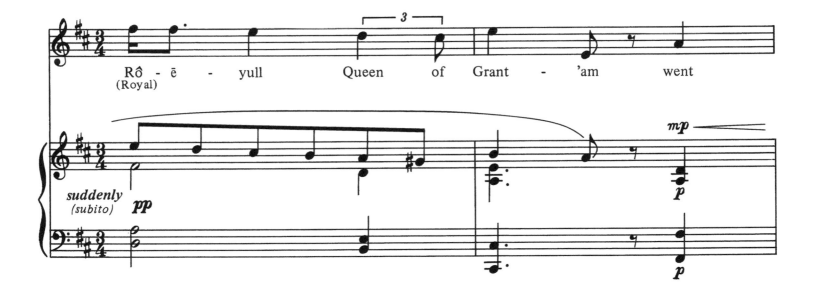

Rô - ē - yull   Queen   of   Grant - 'am   went
(Royal)

suddenly **pp**
(subito)

plenty (molto)   **p** (or **pp**)

weep _ _ _ _ _ _ _ _ _ _ _ _ _ in'   a - wä.
(away)

mf

p

pp

BRITISH FOLK-MUSIC SETTINGS

(Lovingly and reverently dedicated to the memory of Edvard Grieg)

Nr. 24. "THE SPRIG OF THYME"

as sung by Mr. Joseph Taylor of Saxby-All-Saints, Lincolnshire, England,

Collected and set for voice and piano by

PERCY ALDRIDGE GRAINGER

Loving birthday gift to mother for July 3rd, 1920

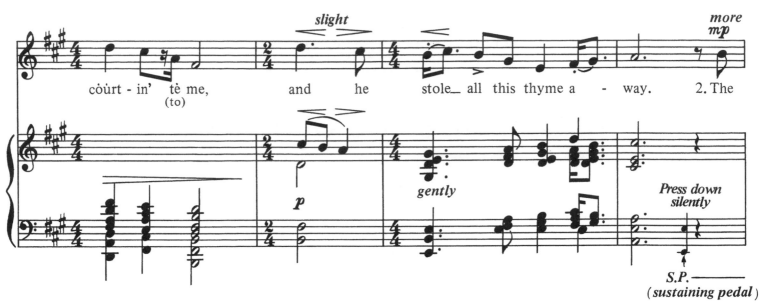

court-in' tè me, and he stole all this thyme a - way. 2. The
(to)

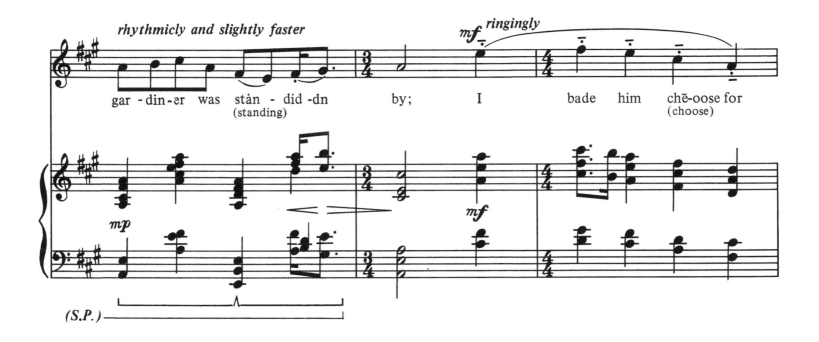

gar - din-er was stàn - did -dn by; I bade him chē-oose for
(standing) (choose)

me: He chose me the lil - y and the vio - let and the pink,

but _____ I real-ly did re-fuse them all three.

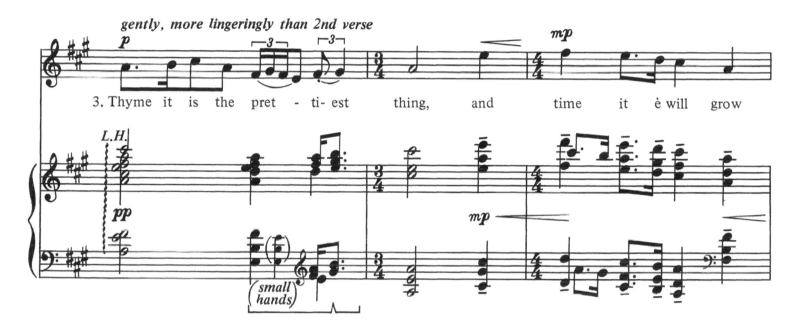

3. Thyme it is the pret - ti - est thing, and time it è will grow

on, and time it - 'll bring all _____ things to an end,

that _____ has won ___ this ___ heart of ___ mine.

BRITISH FOLK-MUSIC SETTINGS

(Lovingly and reverently dedicated to the memory of Edvard Grieg)

Nr. 27. THE PRETTY MAID MILKIN' HER COW

as sung by Mr. George Leaning (of Barton-on-Humber, North-East Lincolnshire)
on August 3-4, 1906 at Brigg, N.-E. Lincolnshire, England,
Collected by Percy Aldridge Grainger
and set for voice and piano
by

PERCY ALDRIDGE GRAINGER

High (original) Key

Set Sept. 14, 1920, New York City
Yule-gift to mother, Yule, 1920

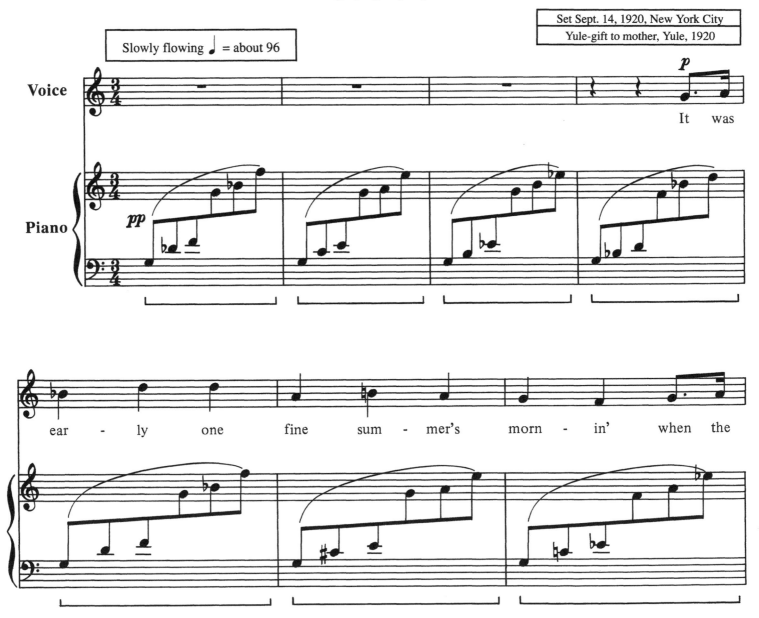

voice so me - lo - di-ous, which made me scarce

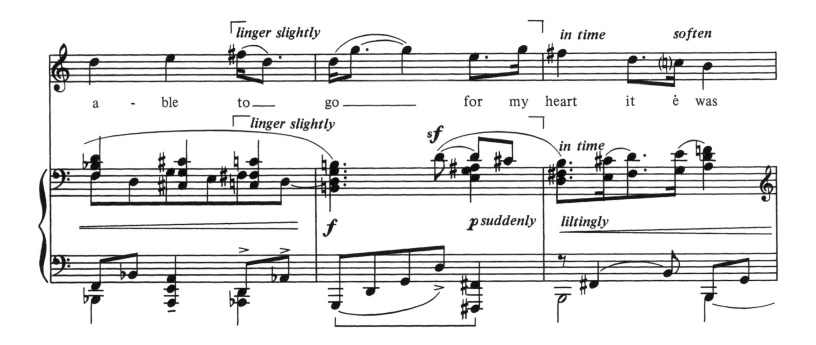

a - ble to___ go___ for my heart it è was

smòth - er'd è with sor - row, by___ the pret - ty maid

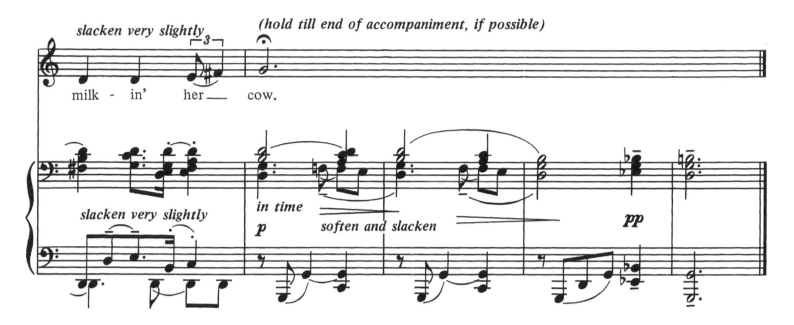

BRITISH FOLK-MUSIC SETTINGS

(Lovingly and reverently dedicated to the memory of Edvard Grieg)

Nr. 26. BRITISH WATERSIDE (or THE JOLLY SAILOR)

as sung by Mr. Samuel Stokes (August, 1906, at Retford Almshouses, Retford,
Nottinghamshire, England)

Collected by Percy Aldridge Grainger

and set for voice and piano

by

PERCY ALDRIDGE GRAINGER

High Key

Set Sept. 22-23, 1920, New York City
Yule-gift to mother, Yule, 1920

sing-ing a song. The song that she did sing, and the

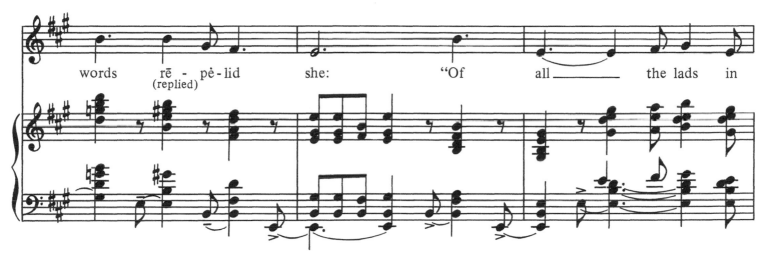

words rē-pė-lid she: "Of all the lads in
(replied)

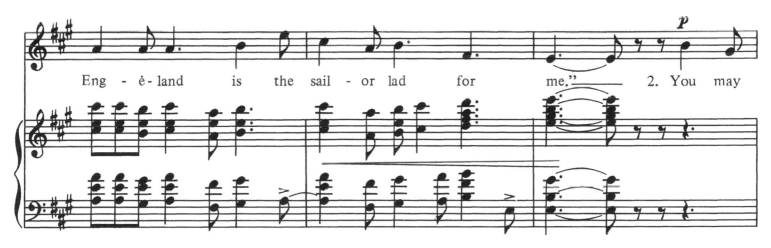

Eng-ė-land is the sail-or lad for me." 2. You may

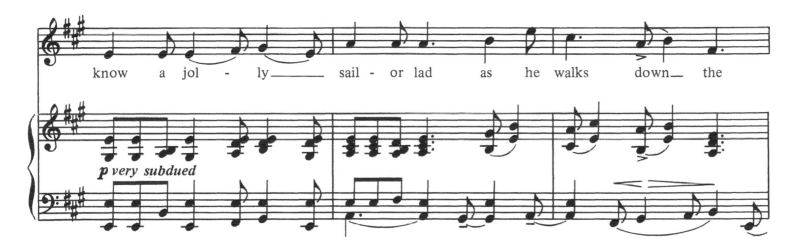

know a jol-ly sail-or lad as he walks down the

street, he is so neat___ in his cloth - ing, and_ so

tight on his feet. His teeth are white as i - vo - ry and his

eyes black as sloes; you may know a jol - ly___

sail - or boy by the way that_ he goes.___ 3. North

Yar - mouth__ is a pret - ty place, it shines where__ it stands; the more I__ look up - on it the__ more my heart burns. If I was at North Yar - mouth I should think my - self at home, for

34

there I have _____ sweet - hearts and here I_____ have got

rough

mp

nōne. 4. I'll go down to yon___Brit - ish wa - ter - side and

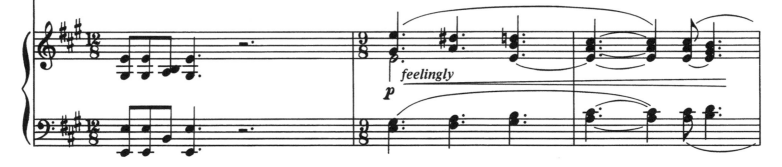

feelingly

p

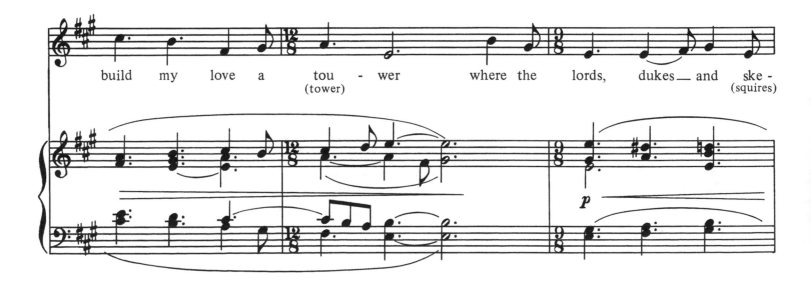

build my love a tou - wer where the lords, dukes___ and ske -
(tower) (squires)

p

wi - ėrs may__ all it ad - mire._____ The

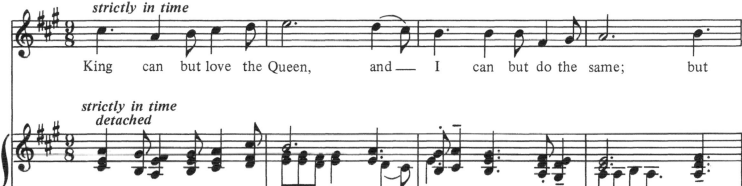

King can but love the Queen, and__ I can but do the same; but

you shall be__ the__ shep-herd-ess and - ell I will be your swain.__
(and)

BRITISH FOLK-MUSIC SETTINGS

(Lovingly and reverently dedicated to the memory of Edvard Grieg)

EARLY ONE MORNING

English traditional song set for soprano voice and room-music (9 strings, flute, horn, double-bassoon at will). Set for voice (woman's or man's) and piano by PERCY ALDRIDGE GRAINGER.

Set October 16, 1901 — August 4, 1940. White Plains, New York.

Set for voice and piano August 25, 1940, White Plains, New York.

Early one morning, just as the sun was rising,
   I heard a maid sing in the valley below;
'O don't deceive me, O never leave me!
   How could you use a poor maiden so?'

Remember the vows that you made to your Mary,
   Remember the bower where you vowed to be true.
'O don't deceive me, O never leave me!
   How could you use a poor maiden so?

EARLY ONE MORNING

BRITISH FOLK-MUSIC SETTINGS

(Lovingly and reverently dedicated to the memory of Edvard Grieg)

Nr. 42. LORD MAXWELL'S GOODNIGHT

Scottish folksong set (1904) for tenor voice (or male unison chorus) and 4 strings (violin, viola, 2 cellos). Set for voice (man's high) and piano by PERCY ALDRIDGE GRAINGER.

Set January 2, 1938

The words in the first half of the tune (bars 1 — 8) are from Sir Walter Scott's 'Minstrelsy of the Scottish Border'. The second half of the tune (bars 9 — 16, 41 — 48) is added by Percy Aldridge Grainger.

Adieu, Madame, my mother dear,
 But and my sisters three, O!
Adieu, fair Robert of Orchardstane,
 My heart is wae for thee, O!
Adieu the lily and the rose,
 The primrose fair to see, O!
Adieu my ladye and only joy,
 For I may not stay with thee, O!

Tho I nae slain the Lord Johnstone
 What care I for his feid, O!
My noble mind their wrath disdains,
 He was my father's deid, O!
Both night and day I labor'd oft
 Of him avenged to be, O!
But now I've got what long I sought,
 And I may not stay with thee, O!

Then he tuik off a gay gold ring,
 Thereat hung signets three, O!
'Hae, tak thee that mine ain dear thing,
 And still hae mind O' me, O!
But if thou take another lord
 Ere I come ower the sea, O!
His life is but a three days lease,
 Tho' I may not stay wi' thee, O!

The wind was fair, the ship was clear,
 That good lord went away, O;
And most part of his friends were there
 To give him a fair convey, O!
They drank the wine, they didna spair,
 E'en in that gude lord's sight, O!
Sae now he's o'er the flood's sae grey
 And Lord Maxwell's ta'en his goodnight, O!

Nr. 42. LORD MAXWELL'S GOODNIGHT

Flowingly ♩ = 84

1. A-dieu, Mad-ame, my—— moth-er dear, But and my sis-ters three O! A-dieu, fair Rob-ert of Or-chards tane, My heart is wae for thee O! A-dieu the lil-y—— and the rose, The prim-rose fair to——

clingingly

friends were there To give___ him a fair con - vey, O. They drank the wine,____ they

did - na spair, E'en in that gude lord's___ sight, O! Sae

now he's o'er___ the flood's sae grey And Lord Max-well's ta'en his good - night, O!___

BRITISH FOLK-MUSIC SETTINGS

(Lovingly and reverently dedicated to the memory of Edvard Grieg)

Nr. 43. BOLD WILLIAM TAYLOR

The folksong was noted down from the singing of George Gouldthorpe (of Barrow-on-Humber, N.E. Lincolnshire, England) and Joseph Taylor (of Saxby-All-Saints, N.E. Lincolnshire, England) in 1906 by Percy Aldridge Grainger, using phonograph records.

English folksong, set for middle-high voice (mezzo-soprano or baritone), 1 or 2 clarinets, harmonium (or reed-organ or concertina or accordion) and 6 strings.

Started dishing-up April 22, 1908, Kings Road, Chelsea, London, ended thinking-out (early June 1908), Kings Road, Chelsea, London. Started scoring August 14, 1908, S.S. Orontes, Marseilles Harbour, France.

Will - yum Tãy - lor, the mã - a - den's nãme was Sal - ly Grãy. 2. Nō
(maiden's) (Now)

for___ a sol - dier Will-yum's 'lis - ted, for___ a sol - dier he 'as

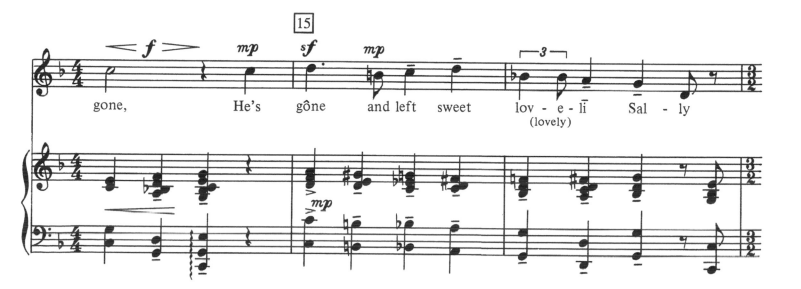

gone, He's gône and left sweet lov - e - lī Sal - ly
(lovely)

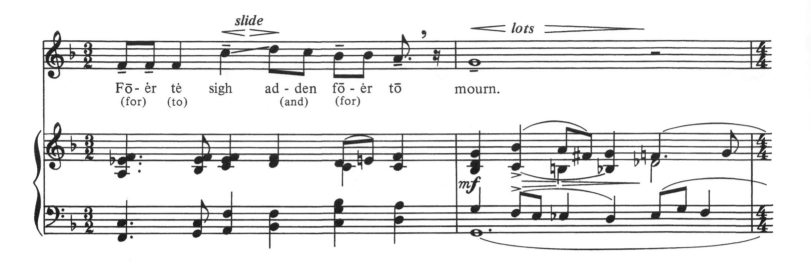

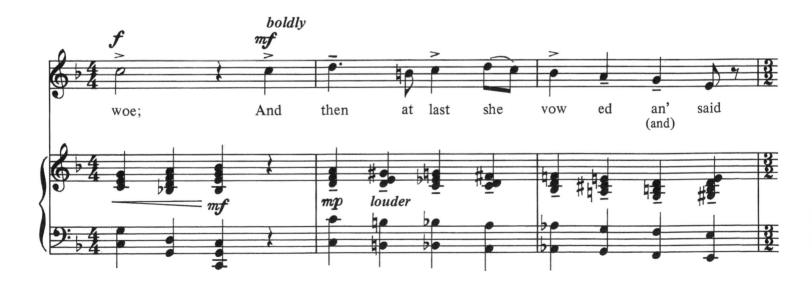

For a sol - dier she wōuld go. 4. She

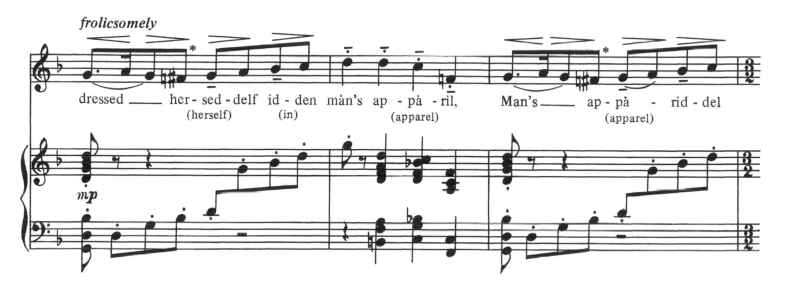

frolicsomely

dressed _____ her - sed - delf id - den màn's ap - pà - ril, Man's _____ ap - pà - rid - del
(herself) (in) (apparel) (apparel)

she pot ôn; Ad - den for to seek bold Will - yum Tay - lor, And
(put) (and)

*Pitch between F♮ and F♯

for tė seek him__ she 'às gone.____ 5. Wôn
(to)   (One)

dāy as she wâs__ ex – er – cis – in', Ex – er – cis – in' a-

môngst the rest, With a sil – ver chē-an hung down her wă-ast-coat And
                              (chain)   (waistcoat)

thēre he spied her__ lil – y-white breast.____ 6. And

*Pitch between F♮ and F♯

then____ the càp-ten he stepped up to her, Äst____ her what____ hàd____
(asked)

brought her there: "I've côme tè seek my____
(to)

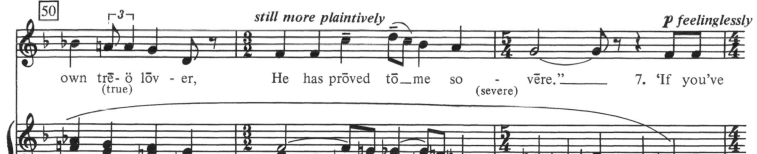

own trē-ö lŏv-er, He has prōved tō__me so -vēre."____ 7. 'If you've
(true) (severe)

côme __ tè seek yèr own true lŏv-er, Prăy tell tō
(to) (your)

*'boddeld' rhymes with 'coddled'

*Pitch between F♮ and F♯

She rose ear-li in the morn-in',___ Ear-ly by the brēk of dȧy, And there she spied bold Will-yum Tay-lor A-walk-in'___ with___ this lā-dy gȧy. 11. And

(break)

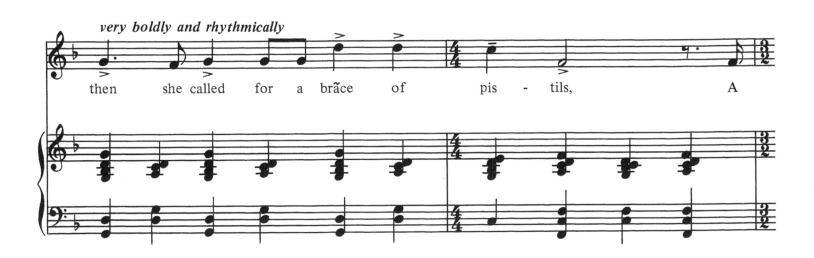

very boldly and rhythmically

then she called for a brȧce of pis-tils, A

brăce of pis - tils at her cō - mànd,_____ And
(command)

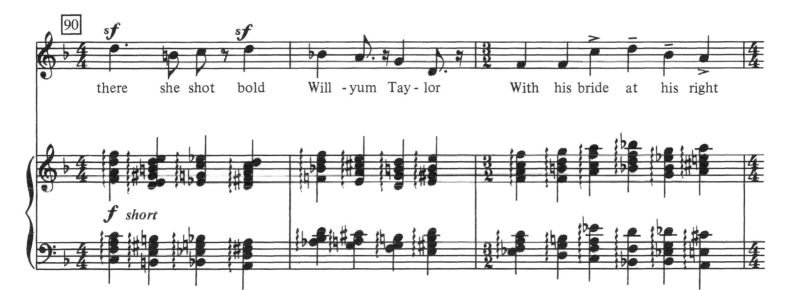

there she shot bold Will -yum Tay - lor With his bride at his right

'and. 12. And then____ the càp - ten he

*Pitch between F♮ and F♯

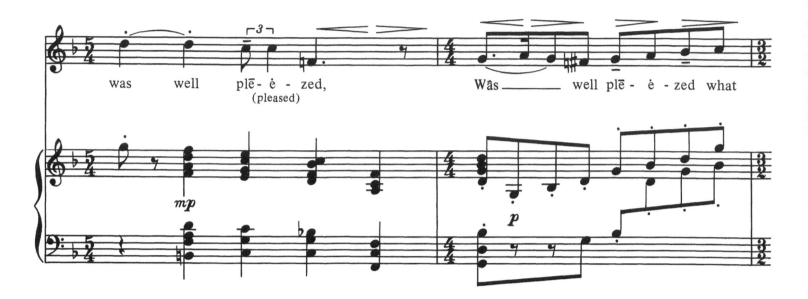

was well plē- ė -zed,
(pleased)

Wâs _____ well plē- ė -zed what

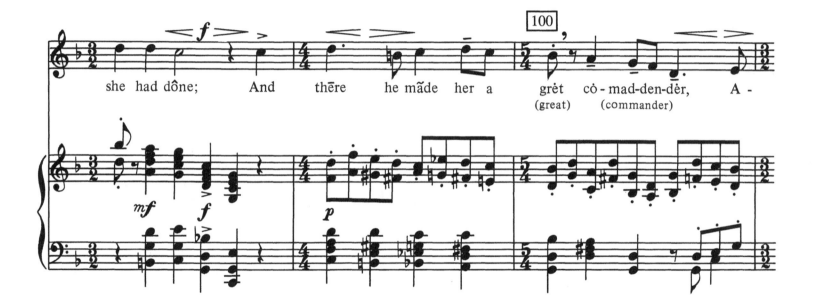

she had dône; And thēre he mãde her a grèt cò-mad-den-dèr, A-
(great) (commander)

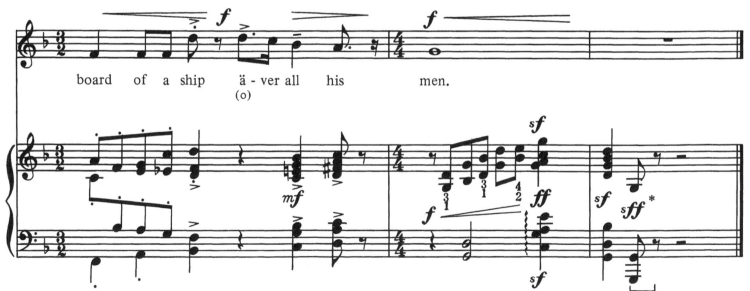

board of a ship ä-ver all his men.
(o)

*Bang fist or open palm down heavily on the lid of the piano on the second beat of the last measure (103). Percy Aldridge Grainger.

BRITISH FOLK-MUSIC SETTINGS

(Lovingly and reverently dedicated to the memory of Edvard Grieg)

HARD HEARTED BARB'RA (H)ELLEN

English folksong sung by Mr. James Hornsby (of Crosby, Scunthorpe, N.E. Lincolnshire, England). Noted down from his singing (in 1906) and freely set for voice and piano by Percy Aldridge Grainger, February 11 — 12, 1946, Victoria Hotel, Chicago.

HARD HEARTED BARB'RA (H)ELLEN

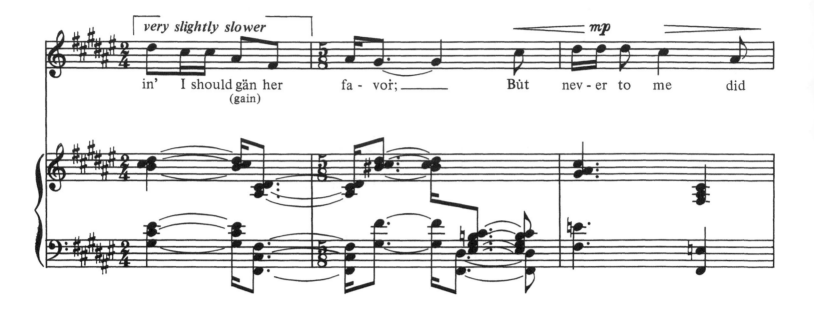

in' I should gän her fa - vor; ___ Bùt nev - er to me did
(gain)

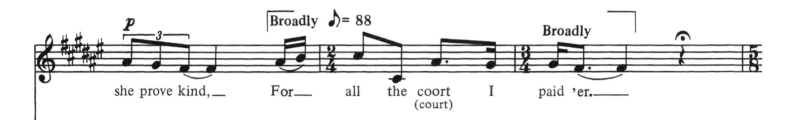

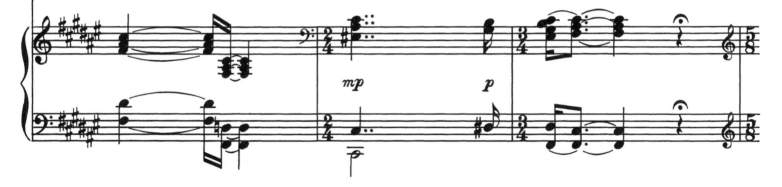

she prove kind, ___ For ___ all the coort I paid 'er. ___
(court)

(Singer follows piano's
rhythmic initiative)

3. Then I

sent a ser - vant to er è house, The house thàt she

did dwel-lin;_____ Say-hin: 'My mas - ter wants tè__ speak with you,
(saying) (to)

If your näme be Bah - brè(H)El - len.'_____

Broadly

Verse 5 may be left out
1st speed ♪ = 120

man, I think you're dy - in'.' 5. Then he stretch - ed oat his (out)

lil - y-white arms, Think - in' to pull her to him; She

Broadly ♪ = 72

turned her back and went a-wä - à. Then he cried:'Hard heart-ed Bah-bre - (away)

(Singer takes rhythmic initiative; pays no attention to chords in piano)

mp (mf) Slowly (about ♪ = 80), free in time

(H)El - len."

6. As she was walk - in' the

Very slowly (no set time)

f harshly

(pianist fits in the chords just when he pleases)

'igh chùrch-yaŕd She heard his death bell tol- lin';____ And e-ver-y toll it

(Ped.) ⸺

f slightly broader

Very slowly ♪ = 76

p (pp)

seemed to sä 'Haŕd - heaŕt - ed ____ Bah - brè (H) El - len.' ____ 7. As
(say)

(with voice)

pp

she was walk-in' the streets a-lōng She met his curpse a-
(corpse)

top voice to the fore

com-in'.____ 'Lä doan, lä doan this curpse of clä, That__ I __ may gaze è-
(Lay down, lay down) (corpse) (clay)

mf impulsively

1st speed ♪ = 120 (Verse 8 may be left out)

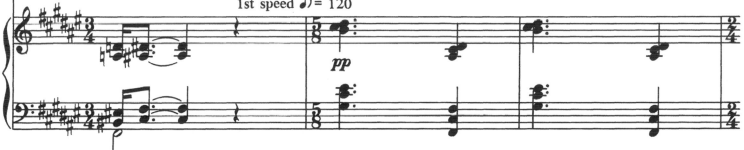

pun 'im.'____ 8. And è when she saw his lil-y-white fáce, She
(upon)

1st speed ♪ = 120

could not for - beer smil - in';
(forbear)
Then her par - ents cried, they

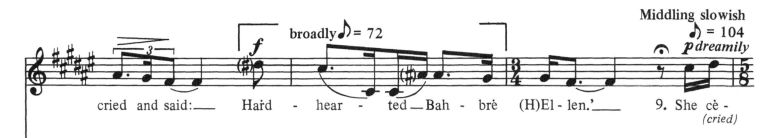

cried and said:— Hard - hear - ted — Bah - brè (H)El - len.' ___ 9. She cè -
(cried)

broadly ♪ = 72

Middling slowish
♪ = 104
p dreamily

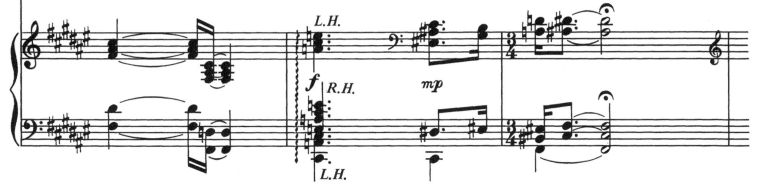

unrhythmically

ried and said: 'O moth - er dear, make

slowly harped*

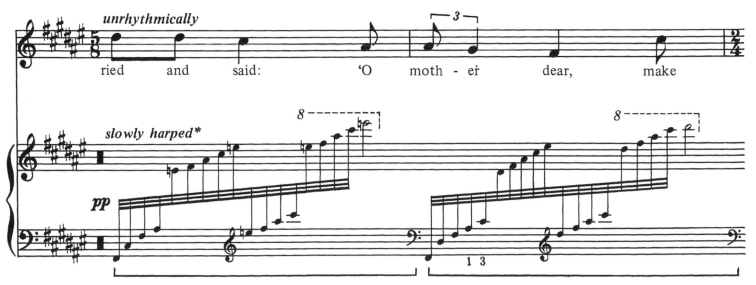

pp

*The voice must keep its own rhythmic initiative. The harped chords do not have to begin or end in any strict relation to the notes of the voice.

me a bed both soft and shal - ler;_____ For
(shallow)

my tree-oo lóve has died tė - dä-à_____ And I'll
(true) (today)

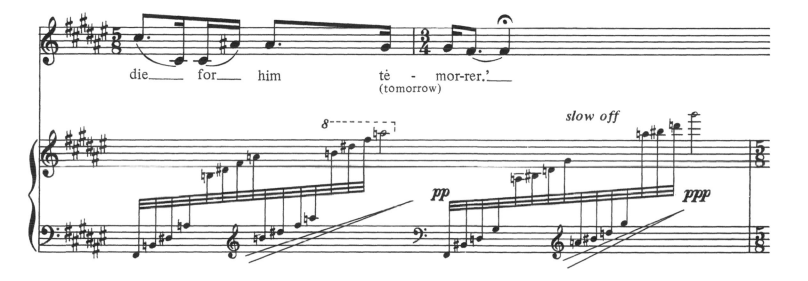

die____ for____ him tė - mor-rer.'____
(tomorrow)

Same speed as last verse

$p\,(mp)$ ♪ = about 104*

1st speed ♪ = 120

p lightly, gaily

Play this passage again and again at same speed (faster than singer's speed).

10. Her moth- er dear she

*The voice must keep its own rhythmic initiative, and not fall into the rhythms of the piano.

made her a bed, Both soft and fit for dy - in'._____ 'For

mf

broadly

O I ree-oo,___ for O I ree-oo,___ I ree - oo that I de-
(rue)   (rue)   (rue)

70

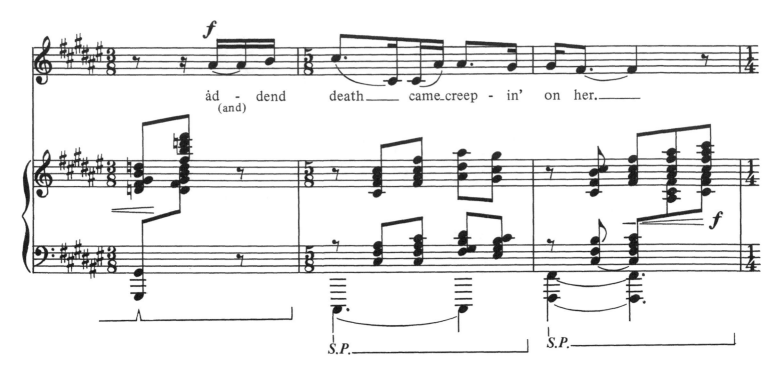

àd - dend death___ came_creep - in' on her.___
(and)

12. The wòn was bur - ied in the 'igh chùrch-yard,
(one)

And the òth - er in___ the___ kwi - er;___ The___
(choir)

won sprung up ä red rose - bùd, Ånd the

oth-er ä green bri - er. 13. Then they

gree-oo and they gree-oo to the high church tòp Ånd
(grew) (grew)

could not get an-y high-er._____ And they

met and they tied ___ of a tree - oo lòv - ers knot Fo - wer
(true) (for)

Slightly slower

all ___ the wur-ruld to ad - mi-yer._____
(world) (admire)

*Taking the last note of a song an octave higher is
a procedure rare with folksingers. Yet so perfect
a folksong stylist as Joseph Taylor does so in
'Creeping Jane', as recorded by him for the London
Gramophone Company. Percy Aldridge Grainger.

CREEPING JANE

English folksong collected (at Brigg, N.E. Lincolnshire, England, on July 28, 1906) from the singing of Mr. Joseph Taylor (of Saxby-All-Saints, N.E. Lincolnshire, and set for voice and piano by Percy Aldridge Grainger.

Loving birthday gift to Mother, July 3, 1921

Sct 1920 — 1921, New York City

Slowly and gently rhythmic, ♩ = about 84.
mp and *mf* in cozy narrative style

Voice

1. I will sing you___ a song, and a ver-y pret-ty one, con-
2. When Creep-in'___ Jane on the race-course come, The gen-tle-men view-
3. Now when that they came to the sec-ond mile post Creep-in'
4. Now when that they came to the third mile post Creep-in'
5. Now Creep-i-n' Ja-ney this race has won and

Piano

Very subdued thru-out
pp
(⌢)
feelingly

1. va - lidd to the worth of half a pin, lol the day.
(valued)

Back to start

2. a - ble for to gal - lop .o'er the ground,' lol the day.

Back to start

3. said: 'My lit - tle làs - sie, niv - ver mind,' lol the day.

Back to start

4. flē - ū past them all_____ like a dart, lol the day.
(flew)

Back to start

5. ōth - ers is not a - ble for to trot, lol the day.

To Verse 6

6. Now

Creep - i - n' Jan - ey she's dead and gône, And her bod - y lies od - den the cold
(on)

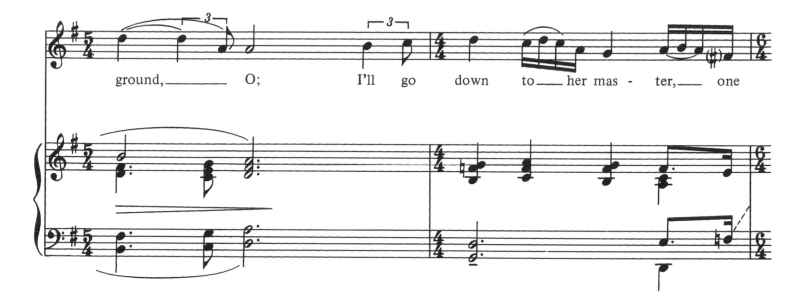

ground,_____ O; I'll go down to____her mas - ter,____ one

fa - vor for to beg; For to keep her lit - tle bod-y from the

feelingly *detached*

hounds, lol the day_____ dē ay, the did - dell ol the

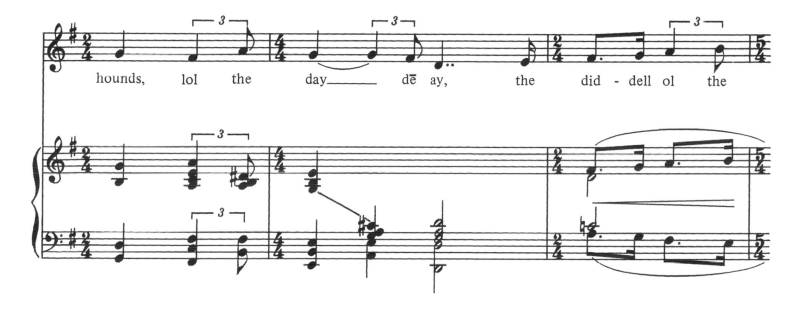

dī dō. I'll go down to—her mas-ter,—one fa-vor for to beg; for to

keep her lit-tle bod-y from the hounds, lol the day.

DANISH FOLK-MUSIC SETTINGS

Nr. 4. THE POWER OF LOVE

('Kjærlighed's Styrke')

Danish folk-song gathered in Jutland (in 1922)
by Evald Tang Kristensen and Percy Aldridge
Grainger from the singing of Ane Nielsen Post,
Gjedop, Tam Soyn, Jutland, Denmark, August
25, 1922. Set by Percy Aldridge Grainger.

Playing-time: about   3.00

Yule-gift to the memory of my
beloved mother, December, 1922.

Set for voice and piano,
September 3 — 6, 1922.

Set for elastic scoring
(from 4 single instruments
up to full orchestra)
Sept 3 — 6, 1922. Scoring
slightly revised, August,
1941.

THE POWER OF LOVE

Slowly, intensely ♩ = about 52

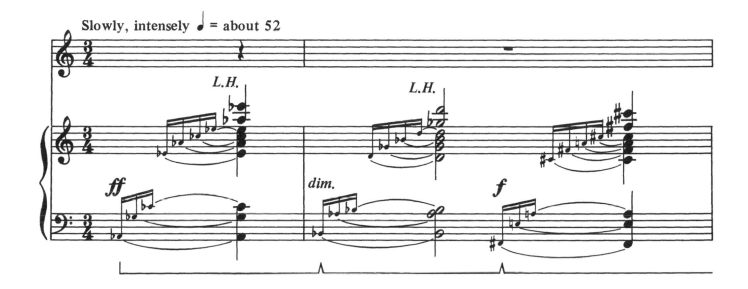

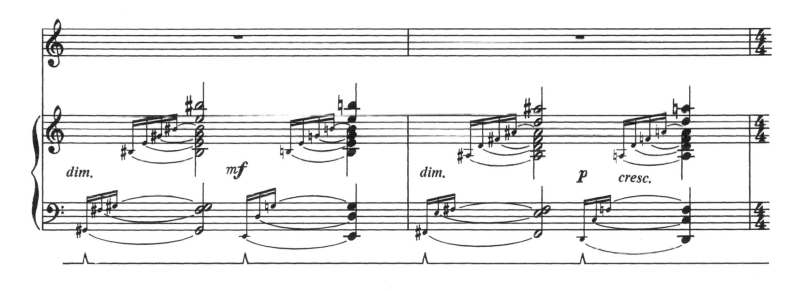

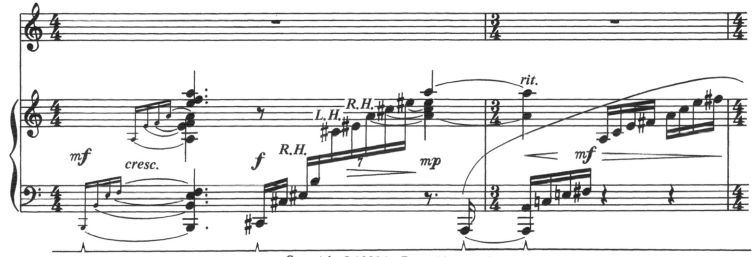

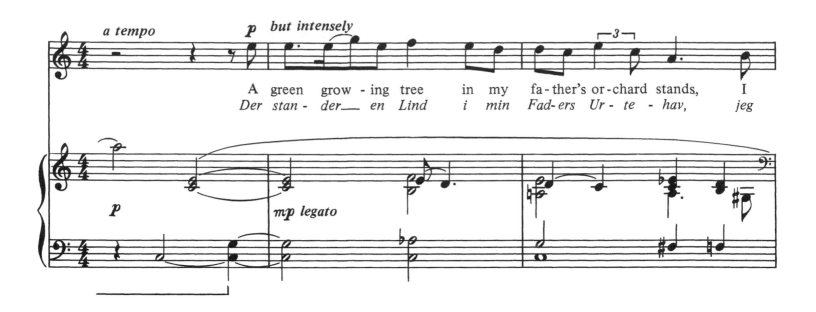

A green grow-ing tree in my fa-ther's or-chard stands, I
Der stan - der— en Lind i min Fad-ers Ur - te - hav, *jeg*

real- ly do be-lieve it is a wil - low tree, Its branch-es twine to -
tror— for— vist det er en Sil - i -je; *den boj - er sig til -*

geth - er so close from root to top, And so do like-wise true love and fond
sam - men fra Rod— og til Top, *saa - led - es gjør og Elsk-ovs go - de*

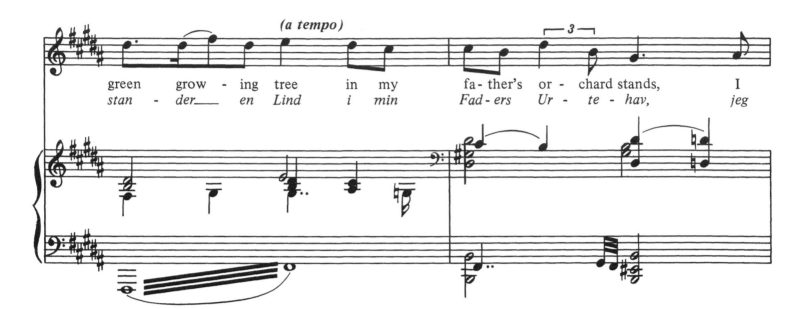

(a tempo)

green grow-ing tree in my fa-ther's or-chard stands, I
stan - der___ en Lind i min Fad-ers Ur - te-hav, jeg

cresc. appass. (rubato)

real-ly do be-lieve it is a wil-low tree, Its branch-es twine to-
tror___ for - vist det er en Sil - i - je; den boj - er sig til-

(a tempo)

geth - er so close from root to top, And
sam - men fra Rod___ og til Top, saa -

so   do like-wise true love   and fond   heart's de-sire   in sum-mer-time.
led - es gjør og Elsk-ovs   go - de   Vil - i - je.   *Om Som-mer - en.*

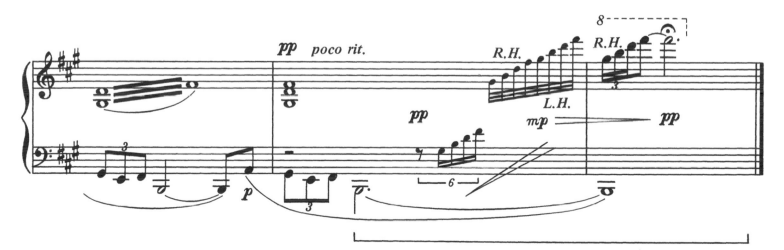